# The Hoarders
Caleb Leow

NEW**POETS**LIST

the poetry business

Published 2024 by
New Poets List
The Poetry Business
Campo House,
54 Campo Lane,
Sheffield S1 2EG

Copyright © Caleb Leow 2024
All Rights Reserved

ISBN 978-1-914914-76-8
eBook ISBN 978-1-914914-77-5
Typeset by Utter

Designed and typeset by Utter
Printed by Biddles Books

Smith|Doorstop Books are a member of Inpress:
www.inpressbooks.co.uk

Distributed by NBN International, 1 Deltic Avenue,
Rooksley, Milton Keynes MK13 8LD

The Poetry Business gratefully acknowledges
the support of Arts Council England.

Acknowledgments
'The Hoarders' was published by *Wet Grain*; 'Singer' was published by *berlin lit*.

Supported by
ARTS COUNCIL
ENGLAND

Contents

5	Our Changelings
6	The Hoarders
7	Archipelago
8	Castle Doctrine
10	Theophagy
11	The Maker
12	The Double's Double
13	Singer
14	Mozambique, 1975
15	Night Soil Man
16	Collectibles
17	Fortune Teller Machine
18	Nativity
19	Microcolony
20	Cachette
21	Earth
22	To the Undergrowth
23	Hunger Pangs
24	Ghost Cities

J'écris en présence de toutes les langues du monde.
I write in the presence of all the world's languages.

Edouard Glissant

Our Changelings

Someone's swapped our sons
for the ghost of Shakespeare again

that creolising crook back in the thousands,
to patoisize, pidginify his own tongue!

Be not afeard, he said, *the isle is full of noises*;
Beknot a frayed, he said, *the eyeless furl of nooses*;

Be now a fjord, he said, *thin icy flows of Norse seas*;
Being's a fraud, he said, *the I is folly or nonsense*;

you can shut one up but you can't shut them all
in my country, home of minor literatures, not even

the English who, horrified to find these
bastards, tried lobotomising their children

to take them back by force! This, I heard,
was what the French did to that rogue Rabelais,

first of the *franco-phonies*, a fitting revenge
for what he did to French while alive:

tried tapping open its brain to get at
the *substantifique moelle* within, put

pressure on the skull of language until it
cracked!

The Hoarders

You   taking up the spade again   you dream of
   something under   you dream of
unearthing   beneath rolling hills of filth
a time before this   the past stretched out
like a flatland   and you'll not stop
   you say   till you've reached the deepest bed
where still you'll find   we say
   our remnants   grafted into the flesh of soil

   this land is rotten to the core we say   this land
on which our forefathers   once adrift
     were welded into place
became the rot under our feet   rose and rose
   into statues   and still you believe
you can raise a spade
    against these fathers   these gods of decay?

every spade   every body   will turn to waste
  we tell you   and when the last of your efforts
are spent we know   you'll flee
   like all the others   you'll run right to the shore
     but know this   we'll tell you this
this empire of scraps   destined to rise and rise
     we'll not cede an inch of it
  our children   our trash we'll
   we'll not let a single one   drift

Archipelago

isle of aporia   isle of brave new world   isle of calibanned   isle of crusoefied

isle of desolation   isle of exiles   isle of first-world   isle of full poor cell

isle of global power   isle of holiday resort   isle of isolation   isle of isles

isle of jubilee   isle of killing fields   isle of little britain   isle of mass tourism

isle of no place   isle of neutrality   isle of outsiders   isle of parasites

isle of queer joy   isle of rags   isle of riches   isle of siegedom

isle of treasure   isle of trash   isle of usurpers   isle of vanishers

isle of western fantasy   isle of xenophobes   isle of yin-yang   isle of zealots

Castle Doctrine

Ascending to safety in a skyscraper
of my choice, I feel a sudden rush of duty
to what some would call *my kind*.
In times of apocalypse, we think
fondly of those we will never know,
thus a decorated duke takes
refuge in my mind: my ancient Other,
most cunning of the courtiers in
his kingdom. He spins me a tale
of a former tower, says it was where
he once cradled me through
sieges long ago. And retreating
as I am from a present set of dangers,
I'm moved by a deep indebtedness,
the thought of my life bound to
his life alone. It's easy to say you shouldn't
live for those before you, but what else is
there to do with no children of your own?
The truth is, I knew from the start that
this man was an impostor; could give me no
name, no face, no written form
of proof. But it was something else he said
that made me want to believe him:
that in these last days, even bastards
might find themselves descended from
nobility of some kind; thus even I,
born to three generations of wanderers,
think this curse of exile was no more
than a trick of global history, a slip

of Fortune's wheel, and moving
up and up I might yet find distant
ancestors surveying me from high up
in their castles, while all around them
lies a landscape burnt and
pillaged and ruined.

Theophagy

The cluster of steeples:
stores of plenty, silos
of blood, stockpiles of
wafer popped for the
ecstasy of the flesh. Past
their pews of slaked and
sated masses: a woman,
shunned, in her room of
run-down deities, gnawing
on painted maidens,
her goddesses of clay.

The Maker

I mould my creatures from a purer kind
of clay. I breathe life into the dolls of

their bodies; my spirit is enough.
They have no need for charms or

amulets, though once – just once – afraid
for the safety of my child, I sent him off

with a talisman carved from stone.
The stone was of the earth, I reasoned,

and could not change the nature of his
being: him, that unadulterated image

of me. Was it the vagaries of new wars that
drove him mad in the end? I blame myself,

nonetheless, for the slow bloom of his
paranoia. For it was I who first planted

the seed of lack in his mind. And now
that fear is his alone; I watch him weld

sheet upon sheet of metal to himself,
my beloved slowly turning into a machine.

I see your body is your armour now and you
no longer need me. Grafted child, come home.

The Double's Double

You were only a clone's clone,
an experiment to see how far the
source code could be corrupted

everything you touched turned to
kitsch or replica: the curse of Midas
cursed by you again

the test was to see what could
survive of Art after time and
time of degradation

Plato, Wordsworth, Warhol –
slow as slow, you set out to
mimic History's great epigones ...

years later you revealed your
Magnum Opus, 'Magnum Opus',
a copy of a copy of your own

people wanted to laugh but
couldn't, since you were only
a joker's joker, a fool's fool

Singer

> Une machine Singer dans un foyer nègre,
> arabe, indien, malais, chinois, annamite,
> ou dans n'importe quelle maison
> sans boussole du tiers monde
> c'était le dieu lare qui racommodait
> les mauvais jours de notre enfance.
>   *La Machine Singer,* René Depestre

Singer, French for to *ape*. The mechanical choir replicated across the globe, from New York to Vienna, from Java to the ends of the earth. Imitation ensembles springing up in the wake of every tour – proof of a universal music!

Sceptics insisted its success was only commercial, said it was the market, not art, suturing together the tatters of our states. Philistines, unbelievers, you've never stood before these glorious rows of seamstresses!

Tut-tut-tut, listen to their stuttering
mouths, their hemming and
hawing, the morse of their
needles, song of dead time
in fugue.

Mozambique, 1975

In his dreams, old Portugal was a
pot of gold. And the scene of
independence kept playing in his sleep.
Cauldron tipping over like a regime being
toppled: waves of riches, floods of joy.
This dream: a cage, a crib he couldn't
break out of. Rocking him through
the last days of empire, rocking him
softly through the fall of the regime.
In those final hours, it's rumoured
the Portuguese flushed cement down
the sewers as one last act of spite.
In his dream, meanwhile, the air
feels corrupted. The pot of riches
has disappeared, his countrymen
gather idly around. He waits
to hear their cheers of celebration:
from the mouths of his people
chunks of concrete fall out.

Night Soil Man

Beneath every clean city   is a flood of waste water
washing over   muddy streets   reeking alleys
the rats and men   of this underground town
it's hard to imagine   we know   but not so long ago
this clean surface   was known as a sewer city
our fathers   lived up to their knees in it
but this was a different time   of course
it was a different time

one dark and chilly night   a man shoulders a pole   with a
bucket of night soil   suspended at each end   he moves
from house to house   his wife and children drifting
through his thoughts   he wonders if this graveyard shift

but it was a different time then   we tell our children
there are no night soil men today   we say
when the last of them   was laid in the soil
every vein and artery   in his body   grew
to the size of tunnels   and his corpse
blossomed   into the modern sewage system

Collectibles

He wore all kinds of prints to please my
collector's eye: floral, gingham, damask too.

To me he was just an errand boy, passing
from home to home to earn his daily keep.

Once a week he came to dust my trinkets,
eyed with envy the station of my things.

Soon he grew to be one with my possessions,
knew the place of every ornament in the room.

Akimbo by the window one day, he offered
himself for my keeping too. Sun-stained

in that light
               his arms like two stiff handles

I saw the full glory of his *toile de Jouy* fabric,
his body gleaming like a rare oriental vase.

Fortune Teller Machine

Not quite *La Bocca della Verità*
but its commercial double: the mask
in miniature, wearing the face of a
false prophet. Even the marble was
imitation, so no truth could issue
from its mouth but a copy of the truth,
you tell yourself, compelled as you are
to insert a foreign coin, to scan
your winning hand.

The machine malfunctions –
just your luck! Has your unreadable
palm short-circuited its speech?
You watch a salvo of slips pour
out in a logorrheic cascade, as
all the world's fortunes gather
worthlessly at your feet.

Nativity

The trench in the earth was their nuptial bed:
my two fathers, caged even in death, bars of bone
now barren where they once bore many like me.
From the nooks of these skeletons that nursed
lost intimacies, I took the fragments of a broken
lineage I tried to piece together again: as if orphaned
acts of love could sprout new genealogies,
push out the severed roots of joy like
a newborn ready to be wrested, arrested again.

Microcolony

From the bronze bowels of the old god they
marched right to the metropole, hollowed out
the stony heart of culture so the dead would
never rise again. Sons split and spread over
the crumbling continent to map its faltering
terrain, waved flag and flagella with every step to
cheer on History's end – for the lifespan of rot
had reached its limit, it seemed, until word came
back from a landfill far away. Pilgrim pathogens
returned with visions of undecayed effigies –
god's latest forms – while their speech, now
petrified, spoke only of *corps, corpus, corpse.*

Cachette

Past the ant nests, the burrows, the catacombs
   the *dédales*, the *écheveaux*, the French drains

Past the groundwater, the hollows, the irrigation
   the Jubilee line, the karsts, the labyrinths

Past the mycelia, the nuclear test sites, the ossuaries
   the pits, the quarries, the rhizomes

Past the scrapes, the tubes, the underpasses,
   the veins, the warrens, the x-y-z coordinates.

Earth

This may all just be rhetoric, take heart. The earth's a
theatre for the untrained ear, and the heat makes for
aural errata, at any rate. Once, seated by a hearth with a
man hard of hearing, I rose to speak, swept in a trance:
He hateth the ether, the rarer art. He that hath teeth, rather eat!
But the tetra-headed language I thought of as a treat
turned out to be too erratic, or heretic, and to stop me
from hassling him, the man turned to threats. At first
I treated him as just another half-witted hater, but as I
rehashed the reasons for his hurt in my head, it seemed
to me he was right by a hair: to call me a heathen rat, an
earthly dirt-eater. I only got here by tearing up the *terre*.

To the Undergrowth

You are the failed mutiny of
life in the shade, a stunted
attempt to outgrow your
oppressors. Day by day
their regime eutrophicates
the sky, and you are all
that languishes below,
beneath the thick blanket
of a civilisation twisting
out its opaque domain.
You are the mirror kingdom
of all things meek and dark;
kingless, you wear no crown
but the crown of thorns.
Ghost of shrubs and lowly
bushes, each resurrection
you stage is an absence
in bloom. For you are the
bare presence that lies
beneath all plenitude,
the sign and source of
Nature's lack; thus overhead,
leaves go on weaving their
own baroque language,
but you are always there
in hiding, the understory
suppressed, the horn of plenty's
wordless wind and shadow.

Hunger Pangs

The ghost of my grandfather flicks on
like the kitchen light at night.
Like a child up too late, in
search of something to eat, he
rummages through the fridge,
padded motions keeping everything
in place. I like to sneak
up on him, cross my arms
like a parent. Toothless while alive,
his gums go on mumbling all the threats
he can in a dead tongue. But dead or alive,
I've never known what to feed him.
I've never known how to appease him.
Alone at night I switch on the stove,
watch him feast on its
bright blue flame.

Ghost Cities

The coastline was littered with carapaces:
not the well-worn hulls of fallen states

but rows of concrete never inhabited;
houses of the unarrived, the pre-possessed,

empty shells in search of living hosts.
They stood unguarded, an idle citadel

waiting to be invaded, so we marched
through the streets like lone barbarians

over blacktop roads unlit by streetlamps,
to see the dull sights of duplitecture,

all that wasted capital of real and unreal
estate. It was some technocrat, we heard,

who'd left behind these untouched ruins, his
botched attempt to replicate the world's

great cities: London, Hong Kong, Berlin he'd
imitated, tried to mosaic together a metropolis

of his own. Of the many sources reporting this
as a failed investment, only one saw how it had

the makings of a city: an emporium dreaming
of its own eventual emptying, artifice of a place

displaced. To tell you the truth, this city was
no more fleeting than my many homelands –

characters, like my band of nomads, with
fates ghostwritten by some technocrat above,

his pen dictating ebbs and flows, the boom
and bust of all the world's kingdoms; his mind

an unpeopled landscape, where every town
was a node on a map to be endlessly configured,

even that old port city I could and
could not call home.